UNSTUCK

UNSTUCK

The Power of Strategy

Dr. LaKeshia Payton

Fresh Air Publishing
Fayetteville, North Carolina

This book is dedicated to every person that is ready to overcome and dominate in life.

CONTENTS

Preface

Powerful! Awesome! Risk Taker! Gifted! Talented! Selfless! Leader! These are all names that a person may be called daily while making a mark in their areas of influence. What is the feeling within when the same person is stuck and cannot move any further? What happens when the same powerful, awesome, risk-taking, gifted, talented, selfless leader cannot move and is STUCK in a place where no one can help?

I am sure that anyone alive who has experienced life can relate to this at some point in their lives. You could be the respected father, the adored mother, the noble husband, the beloved wife, the fearless leader, the friend who is always there, but you have to address what to do when you are STUCK.

This book was birthed from seventy-five feet above the Earth while hanging from an obstacle course wire in the middle of the Appalachian Mountains. As a leader within my church, I was asked to book a women's retreat. The inspiration for the retreat was to coordinate a trip that addressed the spirit, the mind, and the body.

Each activity was strategically planned with an intentional purpose to provoke spiritual growth and an internal transformation. Although I expected a move of God during the retreat, I was not expecting it to be at seventy-five feet in the air and with me alone.

As part of the group activities, the obstacle course was a planned event. The obstacle course had three levels of difficulty. Each participant was asked to at least complete the first level of the obstacle as part of the activity. The second and third levels were optional. Out of the twelve attendees, ten made it through level one, seven went back and succeeded through level two, and only five returned to conquer level three. If I may add, the weather was dreary, wet, and about 65 degrees. The level three course was very wet, rigorous, and designed for a great workout (for only the body), so I thought. I had no desire to complete the third obstacle. As a team player, I finished the first level, and to challenge myself, I went back to the second level course. As a first-timer, I was settled with only completing the first two levels. I zipped from the second course with a sigh of relief and a sense of accomplishment. I headed to the bay and began taking off the harness when a brave soul said, "Hey LaKeshia, let's go to the top one." With everything within me, I wanted to say no, but I had nothing to justify my response. My approach to the course was, why not? I cannot fail or fall. The course was designed to be conquered, and the harness was in place to ensure I did not fall. My thoughts were, what do I have to lose?

As the five brave souls approached the course, two went one way, and the three of us went another way. On the path the three of us took, we had probably seven obstacles on the course, and I succeeded with ease on the first five obstacles. I was between the other two women who were on the trail with me. Before I further explain what happened, I want you to visualize eight logs hanging in the air with a peg on each side of the log designed for you to step on. The eight logs were attached to a rope at the very top to hold them in the air. These logs were movable logs, when you step out on one, you could possibly swing side from to side. As I approached this obstacle, the person in front of me appeared to have jumped like a gazelle through the hanging log course with no problem. Like the previous courses, I watched this same person take a deep breath, and she went for it. This course was no different for her. I was thinking I got this, if she can do it, I can do it.

I took the first step, and I grabbed the hanging log. Due to its level of difficulty, the suspensions loosen further inward, allowing the difficulty to increase. I stepped from the first log unto the second log and third with everything (I thought) I had within, and then finally I made it to the fourth log and found myself in the place I call .... STUCK.

You know that place called STUCK. It is a place where you run to after you are exhausted mentally, physically, and emotionally. The place where the actions you have taken before are no longer working anymore. Back to the obstacle course, there I was STUCK and could not move. I was thirsty, exhausted, my muscles were tired, and literally hanging from a suspension of seventy-five feet above the earth, wondering how I would make it to the other side of this course.

Life has a funny way of showing us ourselves. It shows up without warning, invitation, and unscripted. You wake up one morning and ask yourself. How did I get here? Why did this happen? I thought I was stronger than this? Or wow, I did not realize I made it this far? I did not know I was that strong. Nonetheless, you arrive at an undisclosed location in life and are now forced to navigate the land to discover a way out.

If the place of what we call STUCK were a physical location, a simple GPS reference on your cell phone or navigation system would suffice to help you move forward. Proximal landmarks help further disclose this isolated location, and a few right turns would get you out. But what happens when this undisclosed location is the inner you, just plain STUCK in a place of the unknown.

Does this sound familiar? Are you at a place of the unknown and don't know what to do? Are you at a place where you tried to overcome, but you continuously find yourself in the same place year after year? If you answered any of these questions with a yes, then you are at the right place at the right time and have the right book in your hands to become UNSTUCK.

Introduction

The Battlefield of My Mind...

The battle in my head began. The thoughts started racing in my mind, I began to ask myself, *"Why did I come up here in the first place? I am not fit enough for this. Now you are holding everybody up. There is someone behind you. You are the reason everyone is going to be late for dinner."* I was raging with self-defeating thoughts, which is the beginning of how fear starts to set in and set up shop. Then, I realized "perfectionism" wanted to join the party as well. I began to look around with exhausted muscles and I started to beat myself up about not being fit enough to master this activity. I do know that an attempt to reach perfectionism is not realistic; however, at the time of feeling stuck, I was allowing the thoughts to flood my mind because of what I was seeing and feeling at the moment.

I could have given reasons why I felt like I wasn't successful while hanging seventy-five feet above the earth. I did not train or prepare. I just showed up. I had the mind and the will to believe I was going to conquer this next level, but that was not enough. Because I was successful in conquering level 1 and level 2 courses, it gave me some momentum to move forward with level 3. I must say, the previous courses were without much effort. But the moment I got stuck, all of my positivity, momentum, and previous accomplishments vanished. Then, something happened, and I was able to feel and see hope again.

It dawned on me that I had to open my mouth and verbally speak to my mind. I had to become my own cheerleader. While these thoughts were racing through my mind, the women from my group were cheering me on. The funny thing is I had tuned out their cheers because they weren't giving me the fuel, I needed to get unstuck. It was at that moment that I realized I had to start talking to myself. I opened up my mouth and I started quoting the Scripture, "I can do all things through Christ who strengthens me" (Philippians 4:13). At that moment, I was able to recognize that I had everything that was required for me to get through this level.

As you can see, I was mentally at a place of being stuck. I took physical steps to move forward, but fear was literally there waiting for me, with its self-defeating thoughts. It tried to stop me, but something arose within me and I started speaking what I knew to be true. Imagine if I didn't have the word of God in my heart to speak the truth. Does that mean I would still be stuck and succumb to waiting for someone to rescue me?

The only way to win the battle of your mind is to be controlled by your spirit. If not, you will continuously find yourself at the place called "stuck." You may be asking "how do I allow my spirit to control my mind so I can get out of this place that I am in?" I am glad you asked, let's explore the tools to examine your position and get you unstuck so you can live the life God has called you to.

Recognize the Inner Voice

The average person who is stuck in a place usually looks to others for guidance. Those of the faith community are trained to seek God and ask Him for direction. When we seek God, we will start recognizing His voice within us. This is the voice that will help us get to the next level. However, many choose to seek the advice of others, before seeking advice from the voice that matters the most.

As I was suspended seventy-five feet in the air, I heard many voices from below sharing some very encouraging words. I recall hearing; "you can do it," "hang in there," "keep pushing," "you got this." But in reality, they could not feel my pain. They did not understand where I was introspectively. From the external perspective, the thought may have been, "all you have to do is...and you will be fine." The people on the ground did not know that muscle atrophy had set in. They did not know I was beating myself up for getting stuck in the first place. The battle was not even about the logs suspended in the air that I had to get beyond. It was about the battlefield that was going on in my mind. I admit it was calming to know that I had people rooting for me to experience a successful outcome. However, I needed more than their cheering me on to get out of this stuck place.

There are times when you reach a point in life where no other voice makes a difference, except for the small still voice that you hear from within. It brings peace and calmness to any chaotic situation; however, this only happens if you want it to take place. Listening to that small still voice also allows you to feel encouraged and inspired to move forward. This is the kind of motivation required while exerting energy in areas where you never thought you would happen. This is the moment when you must push yourself to go beyond what you could ever imagine—using the strength you didn't even think or knew you had. If you are reading this book, you are ready to take action. You are actually at a point where a decision must be made and it's imminent for your life's purpose. I want you to believe that God has given you a still small voice that you can trust. Because it is His voice, it will guide you and help you fulfill your life's purpose.

I need for you to understand that God gives everyone a purpose and a plan to fulfill. This plan ties into you, your family, and others. When you choose not to move forward, it doesn't just hinder you as an individual; it hinders others as well, and you forfeit the plan that He has for us. A great way to explain this concept is when using an example of someone giving you a piece of fruit. However, if you don't use or consume it within the expiration time, it will rot. Your purpose in life will rot if you don't fulfill it. As you open yourself up to God and listen to what He is saying to you, He will give you the motivation to overcome anything. Many times, this journey is uncomfortable and frightening because you are trusting that which you cannot see. When you recognize the still small voice within and don't follow it, fear moves in, and outside sources begin to guide your decisions. You may be asking, "how can I recognize the still small voice?" Let me explain.

Have you ever witnessed a parent walking into a room where their child was, and the child did not see the parent come in? However, as soon as the parent starts talking, the child immediately turns toward their direction. It's because their parent's voice is familiar. They recognize their parents' voice because that voice has been with them since conception. The same holds true for God's voice, except His voice has been with us since before we were in our mother's wombs. If you don't believe me, check out Jeremiah 1:5. When we start reading God's Book of Life, we will begin remembering and recognizing His voice, and then be able to hear it within us. This voice will set fire to our heart and our feet.

The voices of family and friends are usually familiar to us. We tend to listen to them when they speak. What happens if their voice contradicts your inner voice from God? Don't get me wrong, a lot of times our loved ones' voices can come from a place of love; however, when your inner voice is calling you to do something differently, you will have to yield to it. If not, you will continue to find yourself unhappy and wondering how you got to the stuck place in your life.

Back to my retreat story, there I was hanging, literally. There were women speaking to me with such kind words, but I needed something so much more. Their words were encouraging and soothing, but they didn't move me from the position that I found myself in. I didn't have an escape button to get out. The only way out was to finish what I started.

We must recognize God's inner voice and know that He has a plan for our lives that we must act upon. My question to you is, why did God wake you up today? I want to know was it for you to stay in the same place every single day? Do you believe God has a plan for you that goes beyond your wildest dreams? If you are "stuck" and you are asking yourself why your life is on a repeat wash and rinse cycle, I need for you to recognize God's Word states, "Never doubt God's mighty power to work in you and accomplish all this. He will achieve infinitely more than your greatest request, your most unbelievable dream, and exceed your wildest imagination! He will outdo them all, for his miraculous power constantly energizes you." (Ephesians 3:20) How do you get past the place of stuck? Avoid the wash, rinse, and repeat cycle. Listen to the still quiet voice within you and believe that God has a plan and purpose for your life. Trust the voice that mimics God's Word.

Recognize I Must Forgive Myself

When we have been at the place called stuck for a long period of time, unforgiveness and guilt can set in. Because Jesus Christ redeemed us for past, present, and future sin, we can rest and have the assurance that we are greater than the worst sin we may have ever committed in our lives. God even has a provision for us. All we need to do is come to Him and repent and turn from our ways. Forgiving is a lifestyle. Sometimes we focus on forgiving others, which is necessary. Many times, however, we must forgive ourselves for not being where we should be in life or for not taking God's Word seriously. This can keep us in a stuck place as the incident is rehearsed over and over in our minds of what we did not do right.

Self-forgiveness is very critical to our walk as the absence of it can yield to condemnation. Condemnation by definition is an accusation or scolding or punishment for a bad act or an expression of very strong disapproval. However, the Bible declares "there is now no condemnation to them which are in Christ Jesus, who walk not after the flesh, but after the spirit" (Romans 8:1). When Christ gave His life for us, He took our sins and wrongdoings with Him and forgave us. It is up to us to remember that when we stray from God's Word, and we find ourselves to be the one to blame, we may become stuck. Remember that no one is perfect, and our Heavenly Father knows this already. Accept His forgiveness for yourself, just as He expects you to forgive others. Walk-in forgiving others and most importantly, walk in forgiving yourself so you can be unstuck and free!

Recognize What Can Kill Me

Suspended seventy-five feet in the air, I recognized I could not live in that place. Imagine me staying overnight seventy-five feet up in the air. I wouldn't have had food, I couldn't take a shower, and more than likely, I wouldn't be able to survive due to the freezing temperatures during the winter season in the Appalachian Mountains. What makes you think you can live in your place of stuck? When you go to bed with worry and wake up with worry, it sets the stage for survival versus living the life God planned for you to have. God wants us to live a life of abundance, so that means we have to recognize we can't fail, no matter what the situation looks like. Because time was of the essence, I knew I couldn't stay seventy-five feet in the air, and I knew I couldn't waddle in self-pity. If I stayed, I recognized my situation was about to get worse. Closing time for the place of business was imminent for the evening, and I knew I couldn't remain there. I finally realized I had to do something, because the place I found myself in could no longer support me. Can the place where you are currently continue to support you? Can the couch support the vision God has for you? Can the abuse in your marriage support you? Can the lack of planning support you?

Ask yourself, "can my current situation add to the abundant living I am supposed to have?" It's time to make a change before another year rolls around and finds you in the same place called stuck. Ask yourself, " if I remain in this current situation, will it kill me?"

In my predicament, I might have been hanging from an obstacle course, but you might be hanging from an unhealthy relationship, a job that doesn't bring satisfaction, the effects of bad debt, and previously made poor decisions that are now trying to dictate your future. The circumstances really do not matter. Recognizing where you are in your situation can give you another level of motivation to move forward.

When we put so much energy into holding on to the thing(s) that will kill us versus that which will give us life, we end up not having the power to move forward towards the things that will help us reach our goals. This is where fear sets in and hinders us from going back to school and getting that degree. Fear may keep us from making a commitment to marriage and starting a family or purchasing that home. Fear may just prevent you from doing the next best thing that will bring abundance to you, your family, and your community. Because it is ingrained in our lifestyle, fear can cause us to hold on to debt and poverty, bad choices, bad relationships, lousy friendships, and dead-end jobs. Recognize you have the ability to exert yourself in a manner that will allow you to use your energy, the breath that God has given you in your lungs, the strength that He has given you in your body, and the movement He has given you in your limbs to fulfill your purpose.

We must recognize that there may be other struggles and addictions that can kill us. For example, perhaps there is someone who struggles with an addiction, and they were saved a few months ago. Perhaps they made an acknowledgment that there is a call on their life. This does not mean they are immediately ready or prepared to go into certain places and minister to others. They may not be spiritually prepared at that point to resist the temptation of falling back into the addiction. It is crucial to connect with the Holy Spirit because He will guide you. He will let you know when you are ready. Just know there are some things we just cannot handle on our own. If we go back too soon, it can kill you. We must be honest with ourselves. We may not be ready to attend the family reunion celebration that is at the club. It is okay to say I am going to pass on this engagement. A disciplined person knows what they can and cannot bear...

Sometimes we choose not to be compassionate or understanding. Because we are stuck in a place of misery, we may criticize people to a point that causes them to digress. When we are miserable, we want others to share in that misery and we do what's necessary for them to feel the same distress. We may not be stuck in the same place, but sometimes we can allow the situation to pull ourselves back in because we cannot figure it out. This is the place where you don't want your situation to kill you. Premature moves can kill you as well as moves that we were supposed to have been taken by now can kill you. What it boils down to is that the lack of disobedience can cause you to be at a place of being stuck.

Recognize I Can Not Fail

What would you do if you knew you couldn't fail? This is how I felt when I was suspended in the air on the obstacle course. I realized that regardless of how challenging the task looked, I could not fail. I was connected to a harness, designed to challenge me, but it still offered some security. I did not know that I was going to get stuck. If I did, more than likely I would not have taken the challenge. Sometimes we are aware and sometimes we are not aware that our actions will lead us to a place of being stuck. While I was going through this adventure and realized that I was at a place of being stuck, I knew I was going to get down, but I did not know-how. I started processing how I was going to get through this situation. I also reminded myself of the reason for me being up there. I asked myself, "What can I do? What would I do if I knew I could not fail?" At that moment, hanging stuck, I may have felt like I was a failure, but I did not give up. The truth of the matter is, you cannot fail at something if you do not at least try. We must ask the question, "Is failure a failure?"

I think about the times when we compete for something. We believe that the prize for the first-place trophy is the ultimate reward, but that is not always the case. Sometimes the reward is building your character, faith, belief, love in others, and strengthening self-love. You can also learn throughout the process compassion, patience, temperance, and your ability to work things out.

You see, our society has us fooled. Everything is so fast and very accessible. We can put a meal in the microwave, and it is done in a matter of minutes. Now with the air fryer, which is impressive, you can cook a whole meal for a family of four in less than 30 minutes. We can sit down at one time and watch an entire season of a show in one day. We can purchase something online, and it arrives within the next 48 hours. We expect communication to happen within social media in minutes. Everything is supposed to happen fast. There is no time to allow for processing and all these things are happening at once. So, imagine the woman who comes home from work with two small kids. She has the air fryer going, responding to her social media, and walking the dogs simultaneously. Is she failing at life or is she managing life?

When failure seems at hand, always remember to ask yourself, "why?" Why did you start the task in the first place? When I decided to take an obstacle course that I had never done before, and as challenging as it looked, I told myself, it will be okay. Regardless of what happened, I must succeed. I must complete this challenge. Now, I did not know a book would be published from this life-altering moment. Did I get through the course in the manner that I wanted to? No. I tried to run through it without the help of that still quiet voice within me. I wanted to look back, take credit and say, "look what I conquered." The truth of the matter is, I did. I just had to pause and know that it's in God's plan for us to not fail. Recognizing that half the battle is knowing that with God we cannot fail.

Recognize the Support I Need

I realized the group of women on the ground were saying very encouraging words. While I was suspended in the air, there were times when I tuned them out and there were times when their encouragement gave me strength to reach another level. There was a time when someone grabbed my hand and pulled me up. I trusted that person to help me. Often trusting others is not an easy task when you have been independent all of your life. I learned that it is ok for others to help you. My sister in Christ was waiting behind me to go through the course. She shared with me that she had always been at a place in life where she was rescued by others. When she went through the course, her lesson was totally different from mine. She had to learn to get through the obstacles without someone saving her. Rather, she had to trust the strength that God gave her. Unlike the sister waiting behind me, I had to humble myself to receive the help and not feel distressed because I could not master the course on my own. For goodness's sake, in my mind, the course looked so small. This was an obstacle course in the middle of the mountains, made for families. Eight-year-olds could do this for fun, and here I was in my 30s, and I was stuck on a course that a kid could flip through.

In my situation, I could not flip through it. I did not have a cape to get me across. I needed all the supportive pieces to get me over the course. A part of me was stuck, and I began to feel like I was a failure. I felt uneasiness because people were behind me waiting to move forward, and they couldn't as I was stuck. So, I began to feel anxious. I began to feel pressured. I was on a retreat with a group of women, and only three of us are now left on the obstacle course in the sky. The others were waiting for us so we could meet for dinner. The log suspended in the air and my ability to reach it were coming between the group of women and dinner. I had to acknowledge that I was in a place of stuck. I did not know what to do. I apologized to everyone for any inconvenience that I was causing. At that moment, I felt as though I was the one in need. I considered myself an independent being and it was not easy for me to ask for help. The struggle of asking for help kept me stuck in that place longer than I should have been.

You see, when I was stuck in this spot, I could hear voices screaming from the ground, telling me I could do it. I was a little agitated for just a moment because I knew that I could do it. The questions were, "What am I to do? Am I getting it? What ideas or suggestions do you have for me?" After all, I'm the one that's suspended while everyone else is sound on the ground. When someone is stuck, sometimes that's the only thing that others can say is, "You can do it." I realized this situation was challenging, and it forced me to think in a way I had never thought of before. I remembered as a kid, I read better when encouraged to read a book with more words. It challenged me to become a better reader. When we are not encouraged to grow, we remain in the same place. When we stay at a familiar level of competence, there is nothing to force us to go another level. I believe some people in our life want to say more. But there are times they do not have the capacity to give you what you are needing to get to the next level.

Hanging out with stuck people will only lead to one thing—You are also stuck. In every aspect, we are influenced by the behavior and actions of the people around us. We learn behavior from one another. If you place a person in solitary confinement for at least 15 days, it can be enough to cause permanent psychological damage. Think about yourself as a child. Your parents may have told you not to associate with certain kids because of their undesirable behavior. They knew that if you socialized with the wrong crowd, you could possibly take on their ways. The same concept holds true with people who are stuck in life and have no goals or aspirations. You tend to take on the same qualities of those people who you hang out with.

You may feel a sense of guilt when you are no longer stuck, and other people around you are still stuck. Some may refer to this as survivor's guilt. There are people who survived a significant tragedy in life. Others may say, "Oh, it's such a blessing that you overcame the devastation." Some of the survivors are the most tormented of all people. They feel guilty when they survived the tragedy, and the other person did not. Maybe the survivor didn't have children; however, the person that didn't make it had a family with children. I can understand how one would feel knowing that they are still here, while the other person met their fate. We can get stuck mentally and feel as though we are not worthy to be alive. Getting stuck happens to us in many different ways.

What if you're the first person in your family to go to college; when you graduated, you landed a good job. Your new financial status allowed you to escape an environment of poverty and paved the way for your success in life. Sometimes guilt may plague and cause the individual to feel badly when they successfully move out of the neighborhood. They may drive a nice car or possess a certain level of wealth that the people they grow up with do not have. From another point of view, the individual may exhibit arrogance or an attitude that is selfish and demeaning. They may have thoughts such as, "You just need to make up your mind to make a different decision and get to where I am." This is not godly. We can sometimes forget where we came from and get stuck in a position of arrogance and pride. The Scripture in Proverb 16:18 reminds us that, "Pride goes before destruction and haughtiness before a fall." It is our position to remember that Jeremiah 29:11

declares, "God knows the plan for our life. He has no plans to hurt or to harm." Therefore, He has no intentions for us to be stuck in any position in our lives. Stuck has many variations; do not succumb to the ungodly plague of being stuck.

I believe the isolation from the COVID-19 pandemic caused many of us to take a good hard look at our lives. We've come to realize that those situations that settled at the bottom of our lives have come to surface. We are now at a point where we have no choice but to be still and look at our circumstances. Look at our situations. Look at ourselves. Look at the accomplishments that may not have been highlighted or realized. Look at anything not addressed that may require some counseling to help navigate through the stuck place. These are not easy tasks and are not for the faint of heart. Most importantly, realize this isn't something you can do all by yourself.

There are moments when you can face the challenges of life alone. Then, there are other times you need someone to help you. A person may come into your life just to get you through a particular situation. Do you know the people God placed in your space to help you? Not by name, but, who they really are? They can be anyone; perhaps, an accountant by trade, and may never need to count anything for you. What are they to you? What do they do for you in your time of crisis? Who is that person when you need guidance? Who was that person with on the weekend? What value are they adding to you? Are they taking more away than adding? Do we have that feel-good friend? Well, their only purpose in life is just to make us feel good, but it's like empty carbs. It's like empty calories. Who are these people? What do they do? Do they help you get stuck? Do they help get you unstuck? Are they planning the next opportunity for you to get stuck? Are they the ones that encourage you once you get there? These voices have different variations within them. These voices sound much different when you are stuck versus when you're unstuck.

Can you tell the difference? Even Jesus had his disciples- Peter, James, and John. The Bible notes about 70 disciples that followed Jesus, but there was great emphasis on the 12. There is a closer annotation to Peter, James, and John. When Jesus was at his weariest moment, he didn't ask all 12 to attend. When he did his last supper, he didn't invite all 70. Can you identify your 70, your 12, your three, or your one follower? Are you able to determine when and where they're supposed to show up in your life? I often talk to people when they get furiously upset, especially when it comes to other people. My question is, why do you get mad when fish swim? Why get upset when the tiger roars? They're actually doing what they're supposed to do. Are you frustrated because something is actually living out its actual position? Yes, as a woman of faith, I believe in speaking those things that are not as though they were. I think that some things take time for them to evolve or come to fruition. There are some things that I have to come to reality and truth with. Some things are just what they are, and they're not intended to change, such as a fish will never walk. A lion will not swim. It is just not going to happen. Sometimes it comes down to being honest with yourself and realizing, "am I stuck in a lie?" Recognize the support you do have to take yourself to the next level.

The Plan of Obedience

Once you recognize where you are, now you can ask God to reveal the plan he has for you to get unstuck. The plan of obedience makes me think about Lot's wife, who turned around, when they were not supposed to turn around, when the city of Sodom and Gomorrah was being destroyed. The angels said don't look back and keep going forward. His wife looked back and turned into a pillar of salt. I think there is a time when we reflect and collect those things that we have forgotten to get in a hurry during a crisis. Sometimes we are supposed to go and not look back. How do you determine what you need to do at the right time? This is the time to ask God to reveal the plan he has for you to get unstuck. He can say to look back or to keep going forward, either one can be completely appropriate, but out of disobedience one of them can change your life for the worse. The plan of obedience for Lot's wife was to not turn around but to move forward. Her life was on the line and because of her disobedience, she died.

Waiting in obedience is not the same as being stuck in the place where we have received marching orders to go yet we continue to stay. A biblical reference in I Samuel 13:8 speaks of Saul, who received instructions from his mentor to wait before he moved forward with a decision. Saul became weary. Saul began to give in. Saul began to feel the pressure of the people waiting for him to make a decision. Instead of waiting, as instructed, he proceeded and decided before the time. What was the cost? He lost everything. That decision caused him to lose his kingdom. That day, the anointing on his life was taken off immediately and removed because of his impatience and disobedience. We must be very careful about what we do with the instructions from God. Therefore, it is crucial not to mute the Holy Spirit's voice in our lives. If we hear and obey God's instructions, things will work out. When we move on our own, there is no provision in disobedience.

Think about that. There is no provision in disobedience. Think about being a child when you made mistakes. There was no provision. That is why your parents more than likely said, "do not do this or do not do that," because there are no provisions to bring you back from it. If all else fails, parents will more than likely discipline their child before they authorize wrongdoing because there are no provisions there. 1 Samuel 15:22 reminds us that obedience is better than sacrifice. It does not always make sense but waiting at a time when you are supposed to wait looks different from being stuck. When you are waiting and being obedient, your strength is renewed. You get step-by-step instruction. You have a level of peace because you want things to be different, and you want something to change. You also recognize that there is peace that passes all understanding. But when you are stuck, you are tormented. You are restless. When you are stuck, there is a lot of pressure. Are you resting or are you restless? Rest is the evidence of faith. If you are not resting, you may want to check your faith meter.

The year 2020 was one of the most vital years of our times due to the pandemic caused by COVID-19. Many people were feeling stuck. They were stuck in the house and couldn't go anywhere. It was causing people to be stuck in one place. Depending on who you spoke to, some had positive outcomes and others had negative experiences. Some people were saying it was a time that they were the most creative. They came up with the most ideas. They figured things out that they never even realized before. They learned about themselves. They learned about their families. They emphasized the things they were too busy to value before. Therefore, we have all suffered a level of stuck. Stuck is not a place where you plan to get to. It is not an isolated incident. All stucks look different. You may be stuck with bad health. Someone else might be stuck in a lousy job. Someone else might be stuck making decisions long term for their life; someone else might be stuck in a bad relationship. At the end of the day, stuck is stuck.

The Serenity Prayer often reminds us of things that we can change, though it helps us recognize the things that we cannot and gives us the wisdom to know the difference between the two. Some of us think we are superheroes. As a big Marvel fan, I think some days I can save the world. The fact that I may only reach one person that day might be the real reality. Sometimes our super strength is just saying thank you to others, saying good morning to our spouses, or showing respect for each other. Remember to hug your children with joy without yelling, withhold road rage while you are driving on the highway, and smile at someone, just to be kind. Those are real superhero traits. Remember this, God will give you the details of your plan. He gave it to Noah, Abraham, Isaac, and the list goes on. This is what happens when you have a relationship with Him. When you fellowship with Him and ask Him questions, He will reveal the plans He has for you. You will never be without the word of God. Since you will not be without the word of God, you will not be without instructions. Obedience brings a life of freedom, a life of abundance. There is no such thing as being stuck when you are in God's plan. Meditate on that.

How Do I Get Free?

In order to be free, you must recognize that you are stuck. Sometimes we can be in denial and think this is the way life is supposed to be. Let's make up in our mind today, that any symptoms will be revealed so they can be released. Below I mention three major symptoms that you must check to see if it is in your life.

Poor Mentality

You may say to yourself, "Oh no, I am not poor,

I am able to eat and feed my family." Remember our needs are automatic provisions, but what about the abundance? John 10:10 reminds us that we are to have life and have it much more abundantly. There is nothing abundant about being stuck in a place that does not add value to your life. There is nothing prosperous about being in a position of "coulda, woulda, and shoulda." You may say to yourself one day, I will think about it, or maybe I will do it. Nothing is happening in that place. Suppose there is no action to move you to the next level. So, I say, poor mentality just leaves you poor. A poor mentality translates into so many other things, such as, poor health, poor wealth, poor relationships, poor generations. It also includes poor thought processes, poor choices, poor attitude, poor cities, and the list can go on. Think about the definition of poor. You cannot do anything when you are poor. When you are poor, you are trying to make it to survive and are in survival mode. You cannot progress appropriately with this mindset.

This attitude is known as the "This is how we always do it; therefore, this is the outcome that we will always get." This is a great example of insanity, doing the same thing over and over and expecting a different result. After all, when you do the same thing, two plus two will always equal four unless you change the variable; in the end, the answer is still going to be the same. You must be willing to change to a new way of thinking in order to receive transformation. Often, we get stuck with a poor mentality.

There are several things that can create a poor mentality, such as the people you hang around, the conversations we have, the things we watch on TV, and the stuff we play in our ears. You have to ask yourself, "What am I listening to? What am I watching on television? Who is around me? What actions am I taking to move away from these toxic behaviors? As a Christian, am I showing who my God is?"

I heard someone say one time, "I know how to eat the meat and spit out the fat." I assure you that even though you might think you know how to do this, there are times when you still get what you do not think you want. The best way to deal with this is to avoid certain areas where you know that do not add value to your life. There are times when we get into positions or get into places where we may be stuck for a moment. But I believe that there is always a way of escape. Sometimes we are so precomposed to what we are used to, even when the gate is open to be free, we will sit and remain in an unlocked room. This is being stuck. We get used to where we are and will become institutionalized in our stuck. Stuck can become common and familiar. There is a lack of grit. Some have a mentality of "all I must do is survive; therefore, I cannot move further." John 10:10 reminds us that we are to have life and to have it more abundantly. There is nothing abundant about being stuck in a place that does not add value to your life.

Religion

Being stuck in religion is an area that plagues a lot of people. Speaking on this topic is not a popular topic. However, it is one of those topics that is often unaddressed but the most elusive. One thing that gets lost in the modern-day church is that there is a difference between God's relationship and the relationship that man has with a building. The great commission requires us to go out into the land and draw men into Jesus Christ. We are to exemplify the fruit of the spirit through our character and draw men into the Kingdom of God.

Let me be very, very specific, and very explicit. There is a difference between the Kingdom and the church building. Now hear me out. By all means, I'm not telling anyone not to go to church or not to be a part of a building. I am saying that your works should draw others into the Kingdom of God. Yes, you should tithe, and you should give your time. Yes, you should fellowship with one another, but if all your work and all the resources are isolated to the four walls, we have missed the mark.

In some cases, we find that the preacher has fallen in love with preaching, and the saints have fallen in love with getting dressed up and going to a building. But where are the works? I say all that to say if you can show up every Sunday and you can shout and you can scream, and you can run but on Monday morning, you do not show any love, any grace, or you are not kind, or you are hard to communicate with and you have unforgiveness in your heart, you have missed the mark. Religion has led us to have memorized scriptures in our minds, but not into our hearts. When we are contrary, or when our actions are contrary to what the word says, we have conviction. We are convicted on the things that we do or do not do or the things that we say, the things we should have said, or how we should have handled a specific situation.

Are you in the word enough to know what should be and what should not be, what is acceptable and what is not? What should we be promoting? Do you have the wisdom to be able to respond accordingly? Sometimes we can get so stuck in religiousness. We get so stuck in a church that we forget to exercise faith, wisdom, and sometimes just good common sense. I am not badgering anyone that attends church on a regular basis as I too attend regularly. Everything that I am saying is an observation of facts that I have witnessed over my years working within the ministry.

Performance is normally required in our jobs. Assessments are used in schools to decide if you progress from grade to grade. But there are no requirements placed on the parishioners to grow within the church. The level of accountability is not the same. You can start in one place and ten years later, be in the same place without applying the word to your life. That is being stuck.

There is no word hidden within or desire to grow in a particular area if there's no conviction. There has to be evidence; there has to be action put into place. We must mature emotionally and spiritually within our faith and practice fasting, praying, sowing, and serving. There may be some forgiveness that may have to be exhibited. There may be some grace that you might have to learn. We have to really check ourselves to see if we are truly walking in faith, which is the way of the Kingdom.

When you are operating by faith you cannot do things based on your intellect. You are to live by the principles of the Kingdom of God. We have to remember that we're in this world, but we're not of this world. We have dominion in the spiritual realm that will affect the natural world.

There are rules that we need to follow based on the word of God. When we follow the world's standards, we contradict the Kingdom Principles and practices. We end up seeing more division than we see togetherness. We end up seeing churches resembling what the world looks like versus the church being the head and not the tail.

As a body of believers, we have the solutions to the world's problems. Our ideas, our willingness, our creativity comes from a place downloaded from the Holy Spirit. But suppose we are limited to our understanding or only what we learned with our college degree. In that case, we are limiting ourselves to what we are here to do. According to Lance Wallnau, the author of *Invading Babylon: The 7 Mountain Mandate*, we all have a mountain that we have to conquer. As a Kingdom citizen, you should be at the top, making critical decisions for every industry that influences the world. We are to walk in favor with grace, but most of all to walk in authority due to the power of God.

There's no reason in the world that we should be people of faith living in brokenness or lack. It is because we have limited God to just paying our next light bill. When He says he will meet all of our needs according to his glorious riches in Christ Jesus, in Philippians 4:19, that means He will supply the resources for his vision that He has given you. Jeremiah 29:11 speaks of God knowing the plans He has for our lives. So that means he already knows what we need here on Earth. It is up to us to believe that He will do more than just pay our light bill. He has given us authority with limitless supply. We should be able to call those things that are not as though they are when things look like there is no way out. (Romans 4:17b) We shouldn't have to be subject to loans and debt and become slaves to the very thing that keeps us from actually being able to fulfill our purpose in life.

You should have goals, and someone should be holding you accountable to your goals. Besides holding you responsible for how many times you showed up to the building this month, my question is "what have you done towards what God has set for you to do? Are you supposed to be writing a book? Are you supposed to be creating a curriculum? Are you supposed to be traveling the world and conducting mission trips?" Someone should be pushing you in your area, but often we get lost being a servant in the church. We cannot do those things because we have to go to several revivals within the month, we have an anniversary, we have an event, or we have another practice. And if we are not careful, we will find ourselves being in church 22 days out of 31 days in a month. When do you have time to do that thing that God has called you to do? When do you have time to move forward, grow, develop, and cultivate in those areas? When do you have time to study and increase your professionalism in your business in your craft? So, as I mentioned before, the church is a beautiful place. But remember, the church is inside of us. The Church lives within us. We come together to the building to assemble and fellowship. You can have a structure anywhere, but the church is inside the person.

One of my favorite movies is *Thor*. There was a time when Asgard was in danger of being destroyed by Odin. The king said "Asgard is not a place, it's a people," meaning if you have the people there, it does not matter where you end up. Metaphorically speaking, you can have a church anywhere that people go. They assemble together for the same common cause. Don't get caught up in the building and what can happen within the building. How will you encounter a fight or counteract any attack that comes from any other sources? We have to get unstuck from religiosity and realize that there's a kingdom that's at hand. That kingdom is the Kingdom of God that should be here on Earth. In this Kingdom, we are royalty, priests, kings and queens. We have authority. We speak those things that are not as though they were. We walk in faith. We believe those things that we don't see but will still manifest, but there are times when you might have to wait.

There may be times you may have to wait for those things to happen, but when we're walking in faith and we know God's voice for ourselves, we will know our mission and purpose for our life. The goal is not to hurt us or harm us, but to bring us to an expected end. So how do you get unstuck from religiosity? First, allow me to note, I am not saying to leave your church or leave the faith. I am shedding light on areas that go unchecked when we get caught up in the day-to-day church and forget what we are sent to do. Therefore, the first thing is to acknowledge that there is an issue. Recognize and admit that there is a place where you might be stuck. Observe certain things, the things that are manifesting in your life. Well, the Bible is also true according to Galatians 6:7-9, "that whatsoever a man sow, that shall be he also reap." If you are not sowing into your vision, or into your purpose, then how can you reap in your goal? How can you reap in that particular area? There is no pie in the sky, things do not just fall out of the sky. I do believe in miracles, and I do think that there are times where something will happen unexpectedly and without any rhyme or reason. I am a firm believer that can happen. But the fact that it is called a miracle also indicates that it is not something that happens all the time and is a supernatural occurrence. It does not occur for everyone because if it does, in that case, it would just become natural. But we work for it; we sow into it. We speak into it, and we make it happen. Then, it comes to pass, but there must be levels of interaction with purpose. There's preparation, growth, and studying involved.

There should be no way in the world that God has called you to be something that you should want to be at the top of your game, and you have to think about it. You put yourself in certain positions you do not want to be in. You want people of faith in your world to be in your life, but you also want them to be skilled. Would you like someone without any knowledge on how to manage finances to manage your finances? Would you be okay with them just saying, "I will just believe God?" If your child was about to get surgery, and the surgeon walks in and says he never been to school or trained to be a surgeon, would you allow him to proceed? More than likely, you will not proceed with the surgery. It is likely that one would decide to go with someone who is not saved but skilled as a surgeon, then the saved person who has no skills as a surgeon.

So, the truth of the matter is that if you want the best for the things you need, why not be the best for others that God has put within you. Do not allow the idea of a word to work in your life. You should instead allow the Word to work in your life, meaning put the scriptures into action. You need to start speaking and believing the words you say, working on your calling, and working on your purpose. You should not look back or give any reason why you should not do it. Unless God spoke a word to you and told you to wait, or hold off, or go next semester, then you should go for what you have been waiting for. Other than that, God is sometimes waiting for us to move, while we are saying we are waiting on God. He is waiting for us to make a move first, so he can open the floodgates to bless us tremendously. To get out of religiosity, we must focus on the Kingdom of God, Kingdom Principles (which is the word of God) and know that God's Word will not return to Him void.

Fear

Fear is the main culprit. If you eliminate fear, the other symptoms will go away. Because we are afraid to move forward, people become fearful about everything. They are fearful of getting married because they are worried that this person will not treat them right. Others may fear that they are not going to be a good spouse. Perhaps, you are afraid to run in the next triathlon because of the fear of falling or hurting yourself along the way. The reality is that something should be considered. Does counting the costs make sense? When fear causes us to stop and not move forward, it is one thing to say that maybe we have not moved on or have not taken that step because of a legit reason. But if it is because I am afraid of failure or worried, I am not going to make it, then that is another thing.

I remember having a conversation with someone one day. They had a brother stationed in Europe for the military. The sibling invited the sister for the holidays, to come down for a round trip. The young lady declined because she said, what if the plane falls out of the sky and I die? The brother pleaded and begged her to meet the family's new addition and enjoy a good time for the holidays, but she further declined. As we continued to talk, my response to her was, "what if none of the things you said happens? What if the plane leaves on time, lands safely on time, and you return safely in one piece? What did you lose?" Because of her fear, she refused to take the trip, and she never got on the plane.

To my knowledge, no planes fell out of the sky during that time that she was expected to fly. There are many times we miss opportunities because we fear something. The probability that anytime a plane flies, a car moves, or anytime we walk or move, we run the risk of something happening. But there are sometimes when we make the threat more prominent than what it is. We miss out on great opportunities and great chances because of something that we're fearing but that just gives it more validity than it has. She had a real concern about that plane. But what if she would have made the flight? What if she would have gotten there and had a great time? What if she would have met her nieces or nephews that she had never met? Just what if. Now, there's probably more to the story, I'm sure.

But the part of the story that she shared with me was, "I'm afraid of getting on the plane." Look at all the things that she missed out on because of fear.

Do not allow fear to be a driving factor in life. Fear can create anxiety and depression. It can also lead to an array of health issues that become very real due to something that was not real. Because in our mind, this is what we think, and it may not be right at all. Even if it is, does it matter? Fear creates boundaries, barriers, and walls that keep you from really getting to where you're trying to go.

Fear does not open possibilities; it counters them. It is the antagonist to faith. Faith allows you to believe in hope for the impossible. Faith includes things that you do not see and things that are not there. Consider that over a period of time by faith, the things that you want will happen. On the other side, fear blocks any possibility or any opportunity for that thing to ever happen. Not because it actually stops the thing from happening. Even if it does happen, there is still doubt that a person will have when fear is the driving force. Fear, therefore, can create an array of unnecessary conversations that make unnecessary actions. Remember, our words have power. When we open our mouths as children of God, when we speak, things happen. Therefore, we must be very cautious of the words that we speak. Because when we say it, it happens. If we are fearful, even if there's something that's coming our way for the positive, we speak against it. If we say things like, "I will never get the job," or "No one will trust me," then it may come to pass. Therefore, if you obtain the things you are hoping for, you are not going to do your best work or internally self-sabotage it to prove your fear right.

Fear will cause you to fabricate your narrative. Fear will have you speaking the same language repeatedly and telling yourself the same story over and over again until you believe that is your true self. Unless a mind-shift takes place, the fear in your heart will become evident and will appear real in your life. Job said in Job 3:25, "that the thing that I feared the most has come upon me." Do not allow the evidence of fear to become your fate because it will later become your reality. They say that perception is reality. If that is what you see, and that is what you believe, it does not mean that it is real. If that is your perception, no one can change that unless you are willing to allow yourself to see things from a different angle or the other way. Perception does not mean that it is real. Sometimes we are closed-minded. We have fixed mindsets and no faith. You may tell yourself, "Well, I only understand what I understand. I do not allow myself to see a difference from a different angle or the other way." In regard to that, you may also say "things are not going to get better; things don't get changed." Therefore, you are always going to get the results that you have always obtained. And thus, you will not be able to be fruitful and multiply. The only way we can please God is by faith. You cannot have faith and fear at the same time. They are opposing forces to one another. If you are not willing to step out on faith and trust, then you are operating by fear. Therefore, you will not be able to try something new. Even if you try something new, you may allow the words in your mind and your stories from your heart to change the outcome of what you actually could have done if you have spoken and believed by faith.

In life, challenges will always come about, but in my situation in the mountains, it wasn't about the log. It was about me. God knew what it would have taken for me to stop and notice what He wanted me to see. At that moment, I needed to see how I approached life and adversity. At this time, my place was seventy-five feet above the ground, but metaphorically speaking, this can speak to anyone in any area in their life if you have sincerely come to a place where what was working before is no longer working anymore. You had the perfect plan. It was foolproof. It was a win-win situation, but with one uncalculated variable, it seems that the game is changed, and all hope is lost. But if we eliminate fear and increase our faith, God's perfect plan will be fulfilled.

The Game Plan of Strategy

Once your mindset has been corrected, and you have established the courage to be successful, it is time to apply the strategies that have been given in this book. It would be a waste of energy reading a book that can help you, if you don't apply any of the principles that were given to you by the author. If you have not noticed by now, there have been several strategies stated throughout this book. These strategies will help you become unstuck in any situation that you are in.

My strategy to get through the obstacle course was to first calm down and speak life to my mind. Secondly, I had to discern the right voices that were going to help me. Thirdly, I had to trust others to help me. When you lay out the steps like this, it seems like an easy task to complete. But when you are in the moment, what is normally considered easy, can seem challenging. Part of my strategy was to take action by moving my leg to the left while reaching with my left arm, simultaneously keeping my right leg stable while I leaned forward. Yes, I know, it sounds cumbersome, but it was worth it as long I got the outcome I was looking for. My mind had to reset to the place it was before I began the course. *What do I have to lose? I cannot fall or fail.* I just thought at that moment that it was acceptable to do what is uncomfortable to get out of an awkward place.

After I got the strategy, I then needed to have the courage to ask for help. Sometimes we do not like asking for help. Sometimes we try to figure it out on our own. However, if you are stuck, you probably did not plan to get stuck. That means you probably ended up somewhere that you had no intention of being, but you ended up there. That means you had no intentions of getting to that spot to get stuck. That means there is a great possibility that you did not come with a plan of action on how to escape. There is a point that you may have to humble yourself and trust someone who has done it before or has been around long enough to give you strategy and technique to make it through. When it comes to courage, you must apply it. You must take action no matter if you are afraid or fearful. That is courage, doing it afraid. As the Nike commercial would say, "Just Do It"!

Getting guidance from others can be a vulnerable act. You can be misled or misguided, but that is why spiritual discernment is important. The ones you should listen to should be aligned with the word of God and aligned with what the Holy Spirit is telling you. Someone can give wisdom based on the Word, but in your situation, you might have to apply a different biblical scripture based on the set of instructions that were given to you by the Holy Spirit. There is power in wisdom and mentorship. You must humble yourself to their teaching and their guidance to lead you to your promised land. It was not until I calmed myself down, opened up my heart, and began to listen to the advice of the people that went before me, that I realized this. Before then, I had already analyzed the situation and calculated what they were saying was not going to work but silly me. I'm the one that's hanging, while standing and watching people on the other side, who have already completed this.

Do not allow yourself to be foolish and miss great opportunities by not listening to those with your best interests in mind. It was a combination of wisdom, self-motivation, and encouragement that helped me get the strategy I needed. All the pieces play a part. Every part supplies the whole. If I had the wrong people talking to me, I would have been angry. It would have exerted my energy. I would not even have the strength to apply the appropriate strategy to get out of a situation that I needed to get out of.

One of my favorite movies is *Vantage Point*. *Vantage Point* shows one single event from multiple angles. Have you ever asked yourself, "what is the vantage point view of my situation? How do people view you when you respond or how you act?" One of the key components to measure a true Christian is to measure them beside the fruit of the spirit. It is said that if these fruits are visible in someone's life, then they are exhibiting the characteristics of Christ. Another thought is that a person may or may not be a Christian with the absence of those characteristics. You see, our journeys are designed to empower others. So, as I am hanging seventy-five feet in the air, I realized that there are people from different vantage points that are watching me. I do not like eyes on me in the first place, but what can you expect when there is somebody behind you waiting for you to move? There is someone in front of you, encouraging you to move. There are people on the ground watching you as you move. You must move. The critical thing about movement is, sometimes the journey is not about the activity that is supposed to happen. There is an end game, but what if your moment of being stuck was only to show others how to move when they get stuck? What is your attitude? The words that you use might be the key thing to help someone overcome their anger. What if, how you maintain your peace, and what seemed like a chaotic situation was the critical component to someone making a favorable decision that day and keeping their cool? Sometimes the problem is not about the situation at all. We can make it into an idle moment by it being all about us—my pain. Look at where I am. I cannot do anything. It's this person's fault why this is happening. However, it could be just the simple fact that you got stuck for a moment in time. Allowing yourself the opportunity to listen to others' viewpoints could be the strategy that you need to become unstuck.

At the end of the day, you have to make a

decision to get out. If you don't make a decision, you made a decision to stay stuck. Not making a decision doesn't give you more time to decide, all it does is keep you in a place you don't want to be.

You may be at a point in your life where you feel like you need to make a decision such as finishing a degree or getting married or wanting to buy a house or making a career change. Suppose you have BUT's in your life. Anytime the conjunction "but" is used in a clause, it eliminates the statement before the "but." There's a justification as to why something is or is not. Until the mindset or idea changes, there will always be a "but" to keep you stuck.

For example, let us explore someone that wants to go back to school. That person may say, "Yeah, I think I want to go to school, *but* I do not know if I'm going to have the time." Although this is a true reality, it will carry more weight than the intended goal. Meanwhile, if that can be rephrased, it may sound like this. "I want to go to school and earn my degree in business. I am going to look at schools that offer flexible class options to make it more feasible to add to my life." Now, you are basically saying, I want to go back to school. Nothing will get in my way. Your words have power.

Another part of being stuck in decision-making is allowing external factors to interfere with your choices. Sometimes it comes down to knowing how to strategize or put some things in place of time management. For instance, using the school example there might be a conversation you want to have with your family or your support team on how you can help manage this time. It is a matter of I do not know if I can do this and go to work and take care of the kids. Well, the question is, how old are the kids? Is this something that they can do on their own? Can you delegate chores around the house to eliminate that stress off your plate to free up the opportunity for you to be successful?

If you're thinking about a career change, some things inside of you may be pushing you to do something different. Ask yourself, what is keeping me from making a decision? Below are real-life stories about how individuals were in a place of being stuck and made a decision to be free.

The Story of Tammy

Tammy was stuck in a bad relationship for seven years. Tammy had three kids with her husband, Teddy. During that time, Teddy was a drug addict, alcoholic, and gambler. Tammy did everything that she knew to help Teddy. She encouraged him to go to rehab to get clean and to get better. Every attempt that Tammy made appeared to be to no avail. If anything, it made matters even worse. At the time, Tammy was not formally educated and only had a high school education. She could barely make ends meet and obtain a job above minimum wage to provide for the family. Tammy was stuck. Before Teddy got on drugs, he maintained two positions and provided a decent lifestyle for his family. However, when Teddy resorted to drugs and alcohol, their lives changed tremendously.

They were in debt and faced with eviction. Together, finances were in question, and they rarely had enough money to make it through the month. On top of that, their marriage was on the rocks. Tammy decided that she could not take any more. She tried to appease him by attending counseling and anything else she thought would make it work, but Teddy did not budge.

Nothing worked. Tammy and her three young children eventually moved in with her parents to file for divorce. She allowed herself the opportunity to be relieved. During the time of being stuck, Tammy did not know what to do. She didn't know who to trust. She didn't know how to talk to their friends, because they were either his or her friends, and things became awkward. Tammy did not know much about life at all. She did not know how to manage money and was required to figure these things out alone, as they had always done these things together. Now with a three-year-old, a five-year-old, and a seven-year-old, she's now left to fend for herself and the children.

As much as she wanted her children to have a connection with their father, she realized she could not make her husband be the father her kids deserved. She realized that was a

> *The turning point for Tammy was she refused to allow her children to grow up in an environment that was not safe.*

choice he would have to make on his own. If he wanted a better relationship with his children, family, or anyone connected to them and their life, he would have to make the decision a priority. Meanwhile, she allowed the words inside her to encourage her and motivate her to move forward. She decided to make a move. For three years, Tammy lived with her parents. It was uncomfortable. After all, she was not in her own space. She was used to being on her own. However, she needed to regroup. During the time of living with her parents, Tammy went back to school. Her parents were very supportive. They allowed her not to have to pay bills or provide food. Tammy became a full-time student. She got an undergraduate degree and a professional degree and began working full time in a career. Tammy saved enough money and purchased a new home in an upscale community. Tammy moved with her family and reestablished the core of her family. At that point, she was no longer stuck. Allow me to highlight. Tammy did not become unstuck the moment that the home was purchased or when she got her degree. She became unstuck when she allowed herself not to be stuck in a situation that seemed unresolvable. After the years went by, Tammy and the children got older, and they moved forward. She reconnected with Teddy. Teddy had got into a terrible situation that would cause him to be in a coma for some time.

He came out with a different attitude and a different mindset. Teddy rededicated his life to Christ, joined the church and became active in his community. Now he serves as a counselor to help young boys get off the streets and into rehab. Teddy built a relationship with his children, and Teddy and Tammy have renewed their vows.

Getting unstuck has many different outcomes.

As mentioned before, we never know what causes us to get stuck. No one plans to get stuck; and getting stuck is not an agenda item. No one wakes up and says, "Hey, I want to make my bed, brush my teeth, put my clothes on, get in my car, and get stuck." No one says that, but sometimes it happens, and it happens more than maybe we desire to. We have to look at the outcome of what stuck can do. Tammy was not only able to get herself and her family out of the situation, but Teddy made a decision as well to not be stuck. Tammy was able to forgive Teddy and helped him during his redemption process. They reconnected with new boundaries, and it strengthened their relationship for the better.

The Story of Eliza

Eliza was a phenomenal kindergarten teacher. Eliza grew up knowing that all she ever wanted to do was be a teacher. She loved to teach little kids, and she wanted to make a difference in her students' lives. When Eliza first started, there was a fire of passion for her career. She was very creative and very open and became a big team player and led her team to higher levels of success. Eliza was a proud teacher. Over the years, her zeal began to change as state mandates became more prevalent. She knew the reason why she got started teaching was to help and serve children, but she was losing her passion and joy she once had in the classroom.

She felt like she had gotten bogged down with the bureaucracy and could not be as engaging as she wanted to be. Eliza realized over time it was not really about just the kids but, she wanted to make a more significant impact on the work that she did. She felt like she was stuck because, in her school, she was the go-to person for everything. Eliza worked for 23 years in the same school and had seen six administrators come and go. Eliza became the staple in her school.

She began to have a taste and a desire for something else, something more. She wanted to get into policy. She desired to draft guidelines for education to help make a more significant difference in the classroom, but Eliza felt stuck. She did not want to leave her school, but she also did not know what to do. Eliza felt that she could not move and that her value was so great to her school that she couldn't afford to transition. Over time as a teacher in the classroom, she began to feel sad and hopeless inside. Until one day, she realized, I don't want to do this anymore and I can't.

She knew she wanted to get into policy, so she tried to join boards and committees to allow her voice to be heard and become an activist for education. One thing she realized is that she could still do that without compromising her teaching career. All she had to do was to become more active in the community. She joined her state's education committee to serve as a voice. She was able to speak on topics and advocate for teachers and public education. Eliza began to feel a level of resolve, and most of all, she began to feel the fire and the zeal that she had before returning. Even though some of the school system's bureaucracy did not change, her fire and her passion began to be restored. At that moment, she no longer felt like she was stuck, but she felt as though she was able to contribute. She realized what she was doing in the classroom still made an impact.

Stories like Eliza may seem simple, but a lot of us feel this way. How many people have changed multiple careers, looking for that place, or that moment, or that space when sometimes it's just a matter of us wanting to do more? It can be a call of what you are supposed to do differently on a different scale.

For Eliza, she loved what she did. She had a passion for what she did. She did not want to leave. She loved her community and felt a sense of belonging and community safety. She had a lot of her needs met by being in this workspace. But it was tough for her to get out the four walls of the building and expand, not quit, not abandon, not stop. In her case she was able to answer the call she believed she had as a community leader and continue to do what she loved to do as a teacher in the classroom.

The world is waiting for you to move. There is someone who is needing what you have, but you have to make the decision to flow into what God has called you to. You have the tools and strategies to transform your situation. It's time for action!

Contact Dr. Payton

For Speaking Engagements & Trainings

Website: **www.pdlcgconsulting.com**
Email: info@pdlcgconsulting.com

Notes